Green dollhouse

Creating a Doll's Eye View of a Healthier World.

Photography by Emily Hagopian

ECOtone LLC
publishing company

Green Dollhouse
Creating a Doll's Eye View of a Healthier World

An Ecotone LLC Publication

For more information write:

Ecotone LLC
P.O. Box 7147
Kansas City, MO
64113-0147

Photographs: Emily Hagopian
Book Design : Erin Gehle
Edited by: Fred McLennan, Jill Boone, Jason F. McLennan

Printed in Canada on Recycled Content Paper

Library of Congress Control Number: 2005928424
Library of Congress Cataloging-in Publication Data

ISBN 0-9749033-3-7

1. Architecture   2. Environment   3. Children

First Edition

Photo: Jill Boone

Special Dedication

Sustainable San Mateo County, San Mateo County Recycle Works, Ecotone Publishing and everyone on the The Green Dollhouse Team each extend a special dedication to our wonderful photographer, Emily Hagopian. Without Emily it would have been impossible to convey the wonderful spirit found in each dollhouse. Emily is a freelance photographer based in California who specializes in architectural photography. You can see more of her great work on her website at www.essentialimages.us.

Thanks a million, Emily!

Table of Contents

Green Dollhouse: Creating a Doll's Eye View of a Healthier World

Introduction

Jill Boone

The Green Building Committee of Sustainable San Mateo County stumbled into the Green Dollhouse Project with creative minds and absolutely no experience in either running a competition or designing a museum exhibit.

Clearly, we needed a good, solid team to accomplish our goal and, fortunately, something about the vision and the enthusiasm was infectious. We started with representatives from a small, green-visionary group in addition to Sustainable San Mateo County: San Mateo County RecycleWorks Green Building Program, Coyote Point Museum, Sunset Magazine, San Francisco Design Center and Jennifer Roberts (author of Good Green Homes). Then each of us recruited more team players who possessed the skills we lacked. The key to our success was our spirited team, our ability to think outside the box and our determination to have fun. Delight has been key – as evidenced in the project, the dollhouses, and then the exhibit.

This dollhouse, built by a team at Goody Clancy, featured unique ventilation and grey water systems, solar panels, and a metal roof. Unfortunately, due to rough handling in transit, these photos represent the pre and post-transit condition of the dollhouse.

We were so excited when the dollhouses began to arrive; after a full year of planning, we were going to see the results of our efforts! The first dollhouse was hand delivered from Japan. Yasuo Tokuoko flew over with his wife and assembled his unique dollhouse in our warehouse. The dollhouse was all white with a natural wood floor made from chopsticks and he carefully unpacked trees that he had carried from Japan for the roof. He explained the concept – this was one unit of a larger building that would have commercial businesses on the ground floor and gardens on the roofs.

The second dollhouse also arrived by plane with its designer, Tony Garza from Colorado. Tony had watched the luggage guys at the airport ignore the prominent signs that said "This Side Up!" and dump the crate on its side. After significant repair, the dollhouse was back together and able to be wheeled out of the crate. It was built in a red wagon, with lots of natural ventilation and daylighting!

Then the dollhouses came in steadily. Many were crated or boxed in unusual ways and just unpacking them was a process of creative problem solving. Many came needing minor repairs, including the Tree Fort's outhouse, which for some odd reason had been flattened while the whole tree structure remained intact.

One dollhouse sadly did not make it through in one piece. The dollhouse from the Boston firm, Goody Clancy arrived in a crate which looked liked it had been thrown around in transit. The padlock remained intact but the hinges did not and, unfortunately, the dollhouse was a pile of boards when we unpacked it. The standing seam metal roof made from Minute Maid lemonade cans was the only piece that was recognizable. We could not fix it and the pieces were shipped back home to be reconstructed. Making the call to let the team know was the hardest call I had to make.

The dollhouses arrived and were unpacked in our donated warehouse space.

For several days we eagerly took turns accepting dollhouses and unpacking them. What fun! When the Animal House arrived, I was drawn again and again to the clever list of "Can you find…?" I loved the belt buckle windows, the moccasin bed and the bathtub made of an old aluminum bread pan painted white with bubbles and all. This entry was another example of multiple living units – a squirrel home, a mole hole basement, and a bird nest "penthouse."

After getting the warehouse set up, and the back wall painted a sky blue, we were ready for the jury. We paid our first bill for the Green Dollhouse Project – a porta potty for the jury! Up until then, everything done on the Green Dollhouse Project was donated service, including the warehouse space.

The 14 jurors came – seven adults, each paired with a young partner. The warehouse was lively, with lots of discussion, smiles and play. The dollhouses were judged on two criteria: "dishy doll dwellings" that hold up to active play and delight both children and adults and dollhouses that offer "great green guidance" about one or more aspects of sustainable home design. The creativity and artful use of green building materials and practices of all the dollhouses made choosing the winners a difficult task. No matter how the scores were added up – and we tried several different approaches – the winner bounced back and forth between the Pre-Fab Modular and the Monopoly Manor – two very different entries. The Pre-Fab Modular consisted of different rooms, walls, roofs, landscaping and furniture which could be built in a number of different designs. The pieces to the house were softly colored in light earth colors and very cleverly fit into the two boxes that held the base for the house. Monopoly Manor, on the other hand was a bright, colorful house made out of used materials. The base of the house was affixed to the inside of a recycling bin lid! The house was delightfully decorated with monopoly money siding, a Wonder Bread shower curtain and hand-painted walls. As one juror said, "this one makes me smile!"

Eventually, the jury decided to present Honor Awards to both entries. During all the negotiations, the children kept gravitating to what we call the Elevator House (but which is officially called Rosaceae Sustainus) to play. So, we had an inkling of which one should win the Kids' Choice Award. The children particularly loved the hand-cranked elevator in the middle of the house. This house was open, making the spaces easily accessible, and it also included a grey water system with shell sinks.

One of the best parts of managing the project was getting to know the architects and students who submitted dollhouses.

From the beginning, I received many questions about our definition of a "design student." Because we wanted the whole project to be educational, we allowed students to be self-designated and we received all kinds of entries in the student category, including one sixth-grade student. Her colorful house – bright turquoise with origami wall paper and foil solar panels – appealed to the children in the jury, many of whom thought that the overall colors of the other entries (lots of browns and natural colors) were a bit boring.

Another rewarding aspect of the project was the chance to work with two enthusiastic graduate students, Emily Hagopian and Katrina Jones. Emily was looking for green buildings to photograph for her thesis project and, after learning of our project, she quickly joined our team. The idea of little green homes seemed to fit into her desire for diversity. Emily is getting her Masters in Photography with a specialty in Architecture and she is developing a love for green building. Katrina is in the Museum Studies Program at San Francisco State University. Developing the exhibit design for the Green Dollhouse Exhibit and being the curator make up her Masters Project. Katrina brought new ideas and energy to our museum exhibit design process, helping to re-energize us all.

Sometimes, as I look around the warehouse at all the dollhouses, I feel like a foster parent – knowing how much time and enthusiasm went into the creation of each house – and I feel the weight of responsibility to ensure that these efforts are now reflected in a special museum exhibit. The dollhouses, after the exhibit tours in 2006, will be auctioned to support Sustainable San Mateo County's local efforts to create a sustainable region and/or they will be placed where they can continue to educate the general public on green building. Opportunities to bid on dollhouses will be announced at www.greendollhouse.org.

We hope that everyone who attends the exhibit or reads

The jury delighted in discovering the details of the dollhouses but struggled with selecting the winners!

this book is inspired to do one thing differently in their next home project. If the Green Dollhouse Project introduced you to something new or made a difference for you, please let us know by sending an email to advocate@ sustainablesanmateo.org.

Each and every member of our team has added something to the project. A very special thank you goes to Stephie of iKorb Inc. who put in numerous hours designing the website and then recreating portions of it as each phase of the project developed. Her skill and upbeat nature made her a pleasure to work with, even when we were on a grinding deadline.

The Green Dollhouse Book is a fitting tribute to all the people who have contributed to this project and to whom I am deeply grateful.

—Jill Boone
   Green Dollhouse Project Manager

Building an Environmental Spirit

Planting the Seed of Creative Design through Play

Jason F. McLennan

This book is for parents and children alike. Few toys are as captivating as a dollhouse because it provides such a recognizable and powerful backdrop for many play adventures. A dollhouse brings lessons home, literally, and helps children make connections between the imagined world and the real world in a way that is deeply rooted. Dollhouses by their nature prompt individuals to ask questions. Who lives there? What do they do? What happens to them? How do they live? And in this case, the dollhouses are special – designed to make children think about the importance of a sustainable life and a sustainable home. The idea of sustainability or sustainable living is a very important concept that should be understood at an early age. Do your children know what those words mean? I believe that this book provides an excellent opportunity for meaningful learning.

think
dream
design

I remember many of the toys of my youth with vivid memory — and, when quiet enough, I can still recall the adventures I lived through imagination — the far-off places, the strange and noble heroes and the fantastic monsters and universes. Certain toys — the miniature castle, boat or dollhouse — became backdrops to the most important of these adventures and, like the set of a theatre, provided the structure for a cast of thousands of characters.

Most psychologists agree that play is essential to a child's development, that it helps shape who we are, what we enjoy, and even what we believe in. As parents we can help provide constructive outlets to our child's need to play, with toys that we select and the lessons we help instill at an early age. My parents urged me to make things and I remember building castles out of old cardboard boxes, with turrets fashioned from discarded toilet paper rolls, and drawbridges held up by string tied to buttons. Even though I also had many 'store-bought' toys, I often

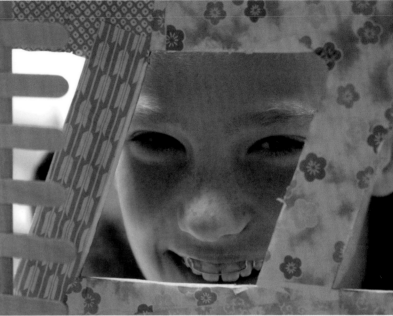

preferred adventures with my own creations – and I was encouraged to explore and invent.

A couple of decades later, I am an architect – still making models out of discarded cardboard boxes, but this time with much more precision, and paying clients watching over with interest. Perhaps I learned some important lessons early on with just the right amount of parental intervention – mostly hands off. Equally important was the encouragement to read – and to try ideas found in books. Frequent trips to the library brought me countless examples of castles to look at and attempt to build. I would draw them, find materials, build them and play with them until they fell apart and then repeat the cycle. How I loved those books!

We now live in a time where children have access to even more toys and stimuli from movies, television and video games that make it all too easy for our children to be passively entertained – to demand instant satisfaction rather than the discipline and imagination required when children are encouraged to explore, read, draw, design and build. Now, more than ever, parents need fun tools to help their children move beyond Nintendo and MTV and find creative ways to express themselves.

Perhaps even more important is the need to find ways to connect our children with the outdoors and nature and instill a love and appreciation for the natural world. Children today spend significantly less time outside than any other previous generation. And yet, when they do spend time outside, they are usually at their most natural and most connected state– at least up to a certain age. Children have an innate interest in other living things; trees, animals, bugs, grass and the like, and there exists great potential to instill a life-long love for the natural world and an appreciation for its intrinsic value and necessity.

love fun laugh build environment

Children are intelligent enough to learn lessons on how their own lifestyles, decisions and actions can affect the environment for better or for worse, and these lessons can easily be integrated into the structure of play for a child. Children are also sophisticated enough to comprehend that environmental problems exist around the planet and how they, through small but significant steps, can become part of the solution rather than part of the problem.

I hope that you, the parent, take this time to curl up in a comfy corner – or better yet, to find a nice sunny spot outside and look through these wonderful pictures with your children. Use this opportunity to learn with them about environmental issues. We have included some fun activities and questions you and your children can both explore as you look through the book. The greatest gift you can give them is your time and interest. If they see you are interested in the environment, they will likely be interested as well. If you are really inclined, you can use found objects to help

re-use
reduce
recycle
play

them build one of the dollhouses and furniture described in the back of the book. Better yet, they can invent, design and create their own.

Most importantly, have fun with this book and your children. This book was created to be enjoyed by children of all ages. It is never too late to build an environmental spirit in yourself or your children.

Let's play.

Fun Exercises with the Green Dollhouse Book

1. Look through the entire book and choose your favorite dollhouse. Why do you find it so interesting?

2. As you look at each dollhouse, imagine who lives in each one. What do they do for fun? For work? Where is the home located? Can you imagine yourself living there?

3. How are the dollhouses similar to your own house and in what ways? What is different? Are there environmental ideas that could be done on your house that have been done in the book?

4. Design your own dollhouse – use pens/pencils and paper to draw the house. If you are interested, mail us a color copy of your design and we might just put it on our website! You can find us at www.ecotonedesign.com. Include your name, age and address. If you want your artwork returned, include a self-addressed, stamped envelope.

5. Parents, help your child safely build a dollhouse from one of the examples in the book, or by using his or her own design. Perhaps you will nurture a future architect, engineer or builder!

Professional Dollhouses: Green Dollhouse Portfolio

The text within this section was written
by each dollhouse designer/builder.

Monopoly Manor

Laura Schwartz & Associates and Murdock Young Architects:
Brenna Smith, Kiyomi Troemner (New York City, NY)

This dollhouse is made from 100 percent reused and recycled material. For example; old vegetable shipping boxes form the frame, there are popsicle stick floors, a *Formula 409* bathtub; *Wonder Bread* bag shower curtain, and *Scrabble* piece floor tiles. Likewise, an apple bottle serves as a skylight, *Snapple* caps function as bar stools, and *Monopoly* money acts as siding. There are *Big Red* chewing gum shingles and film negative solar panels. We built tangerine box bunk beds, a playing card coffee table, and CD case swinging doors. Some items contain points of scale shift — namely, the house cover that becomes a recycling bin, and the compass that can be taken on camping trips.

The accompanying story book, mounted with shoelaces on the side (partially shown on page 70), presents the green architectural strategies used: solar heating, passive solar design, and water collection systems. Willimena the Watchdog narrates, explains these strategies, and the ways they help conserve energy and other resources. She then offers simple suggestions anyone can do to help conserve, recycle, and reuse. For example, Willimena suggests bringing your own bags to the grocery store, and making your next new toy out of recycled items instead of buying it. Some of the dolls also give tips when you squeeze their bellies.

We tried to create a fun, whimsical playhouse that would also make children more aware of decisions they make to help the environment. We hope our house will be a springboard for children and their parents to explore green possibilities at home.

Fun Facts

The Monopoly Manor creatively reuses materials from other objects in its construction, this reuse approach is important in order to reduce the amount of materials that are sent each year to our landfills. Most materials found in our homes can have a useful life longer than what is typically considered. Carpet can be reconditioned, wood refinished and tile cleaned and reused. Or, think creatively and use old radiators as legs for a new desk. www.GoddessofGarbage.com will inspire you!

Pre-Fab Mod Dollhouse

Andrea Traber Architecture + Sustainability: Andrea Traber,
Alexandra Vondeling, Monica Grau, Piper Kujac (Berkeley, CA)

Our dollhouse is conceived as a kit-of-parts, much like a pre-fab modular home, with interchangeable walls, flooring, windows and translucent wall panels. This kit-of-parts encourages children to learn about passive solar design, solar orientation, flexibility of spaces, and integration of environmentally responsible materials throughout the dollhouse and its landscape. The modules are stackable and interchangeable in an effort to make the house kit flexible and interactive to encourage a learning-through-building process.

For superior energy performance and ease of construction, the walls and roof are structural insulated panels. Exterior siding is reclaimed wood siding or corrugated aluminum with recycled content. Interior ceilings are reclaimed wood

decking, and structural wood is FSC (Forest Stewardship Council) certified lumber. Flooring products are formaldehyde-free bamboo, cork and natural linoleum, all of which are made from rapidly renewable resources and low-emitting materials. All coatings are low-or no-VOC (volatile organic compounds). Interior furnishings are made with green textiles. Most of our dollhouse furniture is reclaimed from a previously enjoyed dollhouse, and new pieces are made from green materials. Our dollhouse is PVC-free.

The pre-fab green dollhouse includes a functioning rooftop photovoltaic system to power the ceiling fans, and it will operate in outdoor daylight, with some bright interior lighting or near a sunny window. The roofs are designed as shed roofs with solar orientation toward the south, and translucent clerestory panels for daylighting and ventilation. Our dollhouse has operable, dual-glazed, wood frame windows for optimal thermal performance and ventilation.

Children can also enjoy designing "green" with a rooftop garden for additional outdoor space, and with the deck, can also be used in play, as a landscape terrace.

The site is laid out for solar orientation indicating the summer and winter azimith angles and due south. Site elements include dry creekbeds and a rock garden to allow storm water to seep into the ground, pervious hard paved areas, and ipe, FSC-certified decks. Vegetated elements are drought tolerant plantings that can be watered with reclaimed water. The trees and bamboo planters can be used to shade the south, west and east elevations. Children can also use the translucent panel shade awnings on the south sides to control solar penetration.

Fun Facts

Many wood products come from forests that are not properly managed and cause long-term environmental problems including soil erosion and habitat loss. Thankfully, there are now good alternatives. The Forest Stewardship Council (FSC) certification lets you know that the right things have been done to protect the health of our forests.

An FSC label lets you know that the wood comes from well-managed forests.

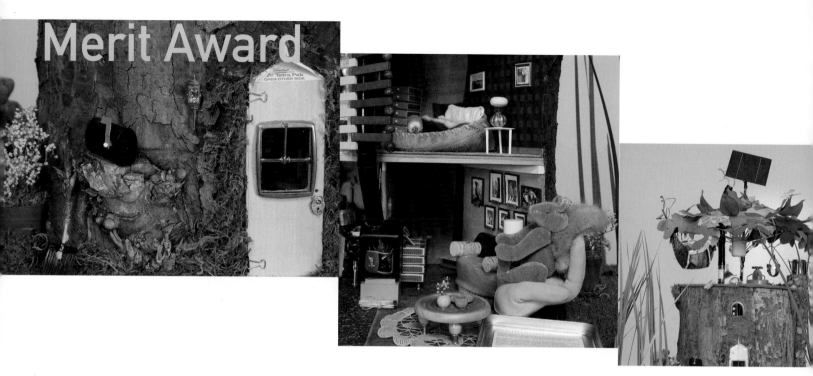

Animal House

Anderson Brule Architects: Monique Wood, Brad Cox, Brad McCurdy, Crystal Melin, Heather Chung, Kate Masleid, Michele Buchholtz, Patty Phan, Emily Cox (San Jose, CA)

First and foremost, this Animal House dollhouse was created from 100 percent reclaimed materials. Nothing was purchased. Only recycled, reclaimed and reused items were harvested for this habitat.

Our dolls are modeled after the Animal Kingdom, because we believe they are our best examples of living lightly, cooperating, promoting and thriving with diversity, and shepherding the earth's resources. Mortimer Mole, Sally Squirrel and Ben Bird have inhabited the earth in a sustainable manner for thousands of years.

The Animal House exhibits examples of solar power (rotating PV), passive cooling (operable windows and stacked plan), solar water heating (PV and water retention), a turf roof, central heat (wood burning stove), water collection and retention (leaves and straws into retention tanks), composting toilet (egg slicer), gray water system (second retention basin), recycling (tubs in kitchen), yard composting and home gardening.

As we have delighted in the (re)creation of this home, we believe that parents and children alike will delight in this Animal House, and discover the beauty of synergy, diversity, conservation, sustainability, and peace. Enjoy!

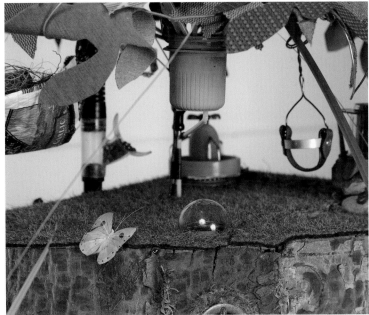

Fun Exercise

Lots of salvaged items were used in this dollhouse. Can you find the following items in these photographs?

Belt buckle

Bread pan

Moccasin

Golf tees

Matchbox

Film canister

Stamp

Milk carton

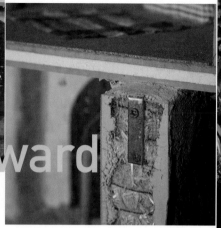

Merit Award

Straw Bale & Half-timber Bamboo Cottage

Hermannsson Architects: John Hermannsson, Lotte Hermannsson, Sean McMahon, Shannon White, Ed Huber (Redwood City, CA)

This dollhouse is expressive of a sustainable philosophy for living. It demonstrates a sensitive and responsible way in which healthy materials are used and resources conserved to enable life to flourish.

More specifically, the dollhouse is green for the following reasons: materials with less embodied energy than conventional materials are used in construction; straw bale walls with a veneer of clay and sand; recycled materials are used – aluminum soda cans for the roof; environmentally conscious materials are used – oriented strand board and bamboo which reduce habitat destruction from logging

large trees; and, an engineered floor structure in a structural insulated panel (SIP) is used to reduce the use of structural material while providing a separate thermal zone at the second floor; clean energy is created with photovoltaic panels that power efficient LED fixtures; and , a healthy indoor air quality is supported with the use of natural clay and sand plaster walls with an OSB floor and natural antibiotic cork at the second floor bedrooms. Bamboo is used for the front door and windows. Curtains and interior furnishings are created from recycled fabrics.

We worked as a group over time to create a healthy dollhouse of human scale, designed to nourish both the body and soul, with the use of simple materials to encourage a connection to nature and a place to dream of sustainable living possibilities.

Fun Facts

Building with Straw is not just for the three little pigs! Straw bale construction is quickly becoming a very popular way to build homes all over the United States and offers excellent insulation values and a good use for a waste agriculture product. Look for straw bale structures in your community!

Kid's Choice

Rosaceae Sustainus

WGS: Roberta Pennington, Leslie Cooper, Paul Gibbons, Natalie Hutley, Liza Meek, Josh Orona, Stephen Price, Tanya Schneider, Debora Souza, Jeff Tathwell, Margaret Ward (Portland, OR)

Definition: A flower of the rose family with the ability to sustain its inhabitants. ("The Rose City," an alias for the City of Portland).

We began our adventure with our Green Dollhouse by selecting a flower to best represent our design concept of "sustainability building blocks." Nearly all materials are from recycled components and found objects, including reclaimed lumber as our building's skeleton and crating system, samples from our resource library, and items from home.

We feel the Rosaceae Sustainus is a learning tool. Five is a number that reiterates itself through natural form. Examples of these natural forms include a human's five fingers, a Starfish's tentacles and, in the case of our overall form, a flower's petals. Perhaps there is no better way to reinforce often "foreign" concepts than by using an ancient learning tool like the number five and reinforcing concepts with everyday objects and color.

Through the Sustainable Communities Network, we found five essential "building blocks" to serve as guidelines in preserving the natural environment for community sustainability.

WATER = BLUE (Kitchen and Laundry Room)
 * gray water reclamation
 * energy-efficient clothes washer with line drying

ENERGY = YELLOW (Dining Room)
 * mirrors and reflective table reflect additional daylight

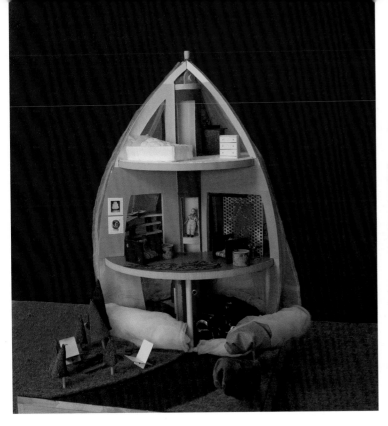

AIR = WHITE (Bedroom)
* translucent petals as the home's covering and keeping core structural forms unobtrusive
* unused cotton squares portray a soft, cloud-like flooring

BIODIVERSITY = RED (Bathroom)
* long-leafed shower curtain, monkey-faced sink, and lady bug toilet live in harmony

LAND, FORESTS, ECOSYSTEMS = GREEN (Living Room)
* tree limb disk tables taken from the designer's home
* fern divider

We employed a few interactive pieces in addition to furniture and accessories to make playing and learning fun. The elevator and the model scooter are "people powered."

Fun Facts

The United States uses more energy than any country on the planet, and since the process of creating energy can affect our water, air and health, finding ways to reduce energy use in your home is incredibly important. It might be difficult to build a hand-cranked elevator like the one in this dollhouse, but you can use compact fluorescent bulbs instead of a normal light bulb and use less energy. Look for Energy Star rated appliances such as refrigerators, dishwashers and dryers to save energy! With simple measures like these, a typical American home can reduce its energy usage by as much as half without giving up any functionality.

Tree Fort
Erlynne Kitagawa, Stahnke Kitagawa Architects
(Harborside, ME)

The Tree Fort dollhouse was constructed from found items, including apple tree prunings, an old rake, rocks, and other natural materials. The underlying idea is that creative play should be encouraged and that toys are best when homemade with found or natural objects. Ideally, children would add stones or other items to suit the play at hand, such as the fork and spoon (garden tools). As Calvin, that boy genius of Bill Watterson, says, "there's treasure everywhere."

The tray base is meant to contain messy things like rocks, leaves or whatever can be tolerated inside. The tree and pedestals are meant to be knock-down pieces that can be removed for storage and glides or rollers allow the base to be slid out of the way.

One of the "green" themes here is water conservation and appreciation. The rain catchment and distribution system was inspired, in part, by the Moorish gardens, where inventive design takes a precious resource and expands and extends its life by artfully slowing and shaping its course. In this case, water journeys from the cistern/shower to a wash basin, drains into a filtering pond and finally spirals through the garden.

Composting, another theme, is a process that transforms waste into an incredible resource. The compost pile is an important element of the garden. It brings balance and aids in the cycle of life and decay. The compost toilet operates on the same principle and it is instructive in that the disposal of our own personal waste is invisible to most children. The vent, wood ash and chips help control smells and aid decomposition.

The final theme here is gardening, the essence of sustainability and caretaking of the Earth. The summer garden is shown as

a traditional Native American three sisters garden of squash, beans and corn. The summer garden provides an example of both complementary food and companion planting wherein plants support other plants. The interior "winter" greenhouse garden extends the growing season and continues to sustain us through the winter months. Both gardens take advantage of a southern orientation and passive solar heating. The stones and hot tub (the giant mussel shell) provide thermal mass to help retain that precious heat.

Growing our own food or buying locally means less dependence on an oil-driven distribution system. Every effort on our part, no matter how small, that moves us away from a reliance on petro-chemical products and toxic commercialism, will help the environment and people around the world (peace not war). Being conscious and aware of our acts of consumerism and their impact is a good first step for both children and adults alike.

Fun Facts

Here's an interesting fact – the average person in the world uses 13 gallons of water a day for drinking, washing and sanitation. In the USA we use 100 times that much per person and, although the earth is 70% water, only 2% percent of that is fresh water and most of that is locked up in glaciers and polar ice-caps. Each of us can do our part to conserve water at home by using low-flush toilets, water saving devices on our showers and faucets and by using rainwater for landscaping instead of water from the municipal supply. Using composting toilets saves even more water, while providing a useful product (compost) at the end of the process.

Green Condo with Roof Garden

Yasuo Tokuoka, Teruhiko Makita, Ziro Mitsumoto
(Tokyo, Japan)

1. Cascading, stair-stepped structures provide seats for greenery and trees to grow. No matter what direction they may face, greenery can flourish in accordance with the given soil volume if structures are not sloped steeper than 45 degrees.

2. Tall deciduous trees planted on roofs cut energy use by maintaining shade in summer and warm sunlight in winter.

3. Canopies are designed to let in light and ventilation and help people enjoy star watching at night.

4. Non-toxic wood floor panels are made from pruned timber. Wall panels are spread with gypsum plaster.

5. The radiant floor heating system is fortified with a zero suspended-particle emission furnace.

6. Worm compost bin helps to dispose of kitchen waste. The worm compost bin helps to dispose of food scraps, which are eaten by the worms.

7. Rainfall and waste water is seeped into the soil spread on the roof garden. Soil bacteria break down organic matter into nutrients for greens and trees.

P.S.
Cascading stair-stepped structures are common on ocean-view hills in the west coast area and roof planting may enhance the quality of the landscape.

Fun Facts

Yasuo Tokuoka's doll condo was inspired by a German cake design, similar to the above photo. This miniature model of the entire complex shows "pieces" of the cake, each of which represents several of the condos built on top of street-level businesses. The flat areas of the "cake" are the roof gardens as shown in the dollhouse model. These units could be built many stories high on the side of a hill and yet each unit would have sufficient sunlight to light and heat the interior. Look for buildings that have both businesses and living spaces in your community.

Play Outside
Tony Garza, Tony Garza Architect (Denver, CO)

Green Strategy: Basic Passive Solar Design
Green Thinking: Play Outside

Sustainable Elements: Recycled and reclaimed wood and glass, solar panels, natural ground floor cooling and insulation, bamboo panels.

The construction of the dollhouse is based on the fundamental elements of passive solar design. The open floor plan, the exposed floor surface, generous roof overhangs, roof pitch, and the clerestory windows that promote optimum heat and cooling distribution work together to achieve the benefits of direct gain. The materials are used sparingly and efficiently as illustrated in the simplified floor plan. The lower floor is left with few barriers between the adjacent rooms and the outdoors. Fewer walls translate to less building material and less energy expenditure. The lower floor lends itself best to public activities and the upper floor creates personal spaces with great views to the site. The public and personal spaces are connected through light wells that carry the brightness of the day into the house.

A good way to learn the benefits of being "green" is through playing "green." The transportable wagon base of the dollhouse is meant to entice children to play outside and to be in the natural environment. The solar pv cell mounted to the roof provides positive feedback when placed directly in the path of the sun.

Discovering the benefits of nature can be lasting.

Fun Facts

Using the sun for winter heat and daylight is an important component of any green building. It is fascinating that daylight may help boost student grades while also saving energy. The Seattle School District, under a study commissioned by the PG&E utility, found student grades increased about 10 percent following improvement in daylighting to buildings studied. People are healthier and more alert when daylight is present!

El Salvage-a-Door

Raphael Sperry, Richard Parker, Adam Weiss, 450 Architects
(San Francisco, CA)

A building salvage yard is a great place for dollhouses! In this house, the base and floor are half of a dutch door (one recessed panel forms a "sunken living room"), and the ceiling beams are off-cuts from the same door. The structure uses reclaimed roof tiles, stair balusters (used as structural columns), a used shelving board (stairs), and used wood siding (half of second floor). The "stripey" and "speckly" half of the second floor is Kirei board, made of pressed sorghum grain straw with nontoxic adhesives. This off-cut was graciously donated by the manufacturer (thanks to www.kireiusa.com). The real linoleum flooring and woven sisal area rug (it's a plant fiber) are healthy, green materials from the sample library where I work.

Doll-sized straw-bales just were not available for the exterior walls, so I developed a simulated cob (or straw-clay) mixture of real straw, gypsum plaster (which dries faster than clay, and is nontoxic artist's plaster), and perlite (lightweight pumice pebbles). I love the rough texture of the outside and the smooth texture on the inside that came from the casting process!

If "El Salvage-a-Door" was a real house, it would collect winter heat, and the roof overhang and lower awning would keep the house cool in summer. The solar-panel awning sports real PV (photovoltaic) material (from an architect's sample) supported on used cassette boxes that allow its angle to be adjusted seasonally. For real energy efficiency, you would want well-insulated windows with all that glass! Well, you would want furniture and curtains and lights and appliances too; so take dolly to the thrift store or salvage yard near you for some recycled additions. Enjoy!

Fun Facts

The average American household spends $1500 a year on energy bills alone. Energy saving features such as good windows, insulation and mechanical equipment can save a homeowner a great deal of money over the life of the home. A passive solar home with thermal mass can also greatly cut winter heating bills. Thermal mass is any "heavy" building material such as stone, brick, concrete or tile that has the ability to store heat. The dollhouse shown here uses thermal mass in its materials. Can you find the materials that are thermally massive? The dollhouse on page 26 also uses thermal mass in an interesting way – see if you can spot it!

Remodeled Dollhouse

URS Corporation: Manda Magee, Ryan Archer, Juli Castillo, Andrew Howard, Susan Priest (Grand Rapids, MI)

The house started as an existing design and the design was modified to incorporate green features. Instead of designing the entire house to be "Green," the team decided to focus on four components, starting with the most difficult and costly and ending with the easiest and cheapest to implement.

The first and most prominent feature is the green roof. The original peaked roof was removed and a parapet was added for safety. The "Green Roof" system was then installed along with the greenhouse for gardening. The garden was included to reduce storm water discharged from the site.

The second feature is the "Living Machine System" partially displayed by the plant pod in the greenhouse. The Living Machine converts the wastewater from the house to gray

water that can be used for plant irrigation on the roof. The remaining portions of the Living Machine System are explained in the education board attached to the house.

The third feature is the use of Low Volatile Organic Compounds (VOC) paint in the interior of the house. This paint is a very easy green feature to incorporate. Reduction of VOC's improves the indoor air quality of the home.

The fourth and final feature of purchasing "Green Power," while not included in the dollhouse construction, is included in the education board.

Fun Facts

Green Rooftops offer multiple environmental benefits including reducing the amount of storm water runoff that is generated when it rains and providing rooftop habitat. In addition, green roofs can be an important strategy in reducing what is known as the "Urban Heat Island Effect" where temperatures in town can be much higher than temperatures in the surrounding countryside. Rooftops and roadways can be up to 50-70 degrees warmer than the ambient air temperature. If you have a green or "cool roof" you will help your home stay cool and decrease the need for air conditioning.

Design Student Dollhouses: Green Dollhouse Portfolio

The text within this section was written
by each dollhouse designer/builder.

Honor Award

Mobile Living

Matt Russell, Loni Sullivan, Peter Zychowski; University of Colorado at Boulder (Boulder, CO)

The design goal of this dollhouse was to teach reuse, recycling and the power of solar energy to children. The materials we used are recycled materials, waste from the architectural studio, and materials that are made from waste and/or sustainable grown materials. The core of the dollhouse is made out of gridcore, which is a material made out of recycled paper. The wheels are from old rollerblades, the stairs are made out of sunflower board, the walls are strawboard, and the carpet is waste carpet which was found at a local carpet store. Borco and origami paper are used as wall finishes for the interior of the house. The exterior walls are painted red with a wash of acrylic paint. The wall sconces light up using the photovoltaic panels on the side of the dollhouse. The round photovoltaic panel on the top of the house runs a fan that is located between the greenhouse

and the rest of the house. The "tub" on the top is used to show that water could be collected and distributed to the greenhouse. The carpet symbolizes zero-landscaping and a place for dolls to play and relax. All of the furniture is made out of household waste. The chairs are made up of old caps, the day bed is made out of straws, the table is made out of CD's, and the green shelves are made out of medical caps.

Fun Facts

Photovoltaic panels, otherwise known as PV, convert sunlight to electricity with no harmful by-products. PV panels typically convert between 9% and 15% of the available sunlight to electricity. A typical single-family home with a roof that is oriented to the south could be completely solar powered by installing PV on its roof. If batteries are added, the system will power the home during blackouts or disasters.

Merit Award

The Bamboo Loft

Rosie Hanna, Joanna Manders, Christine Miller, California College of the Arts (San Francisco, CA)

- Main Frame of House: Bamboo is a highly renewable resource that is extremely durable and provides a rigid structure. Additional exterior walls are made out of ecoresin. The house has a simple floor plan in order not to detract from the beauty of materials used.

- Larger Spaces for Play: The rooms of the house are larger and more modern because of raised ceilings. Because the house is open on all four sides, more than one child can play with the house at a time.

- Unexpected Structural Elements: A "green roof" with grass and shrubbery encourages green building. Polartec fleece (made from recycled plastic) is used to represent grass and leaves.

- Nature as a Focal Point: A large tree running through a quarter of the house encourages the idea of clean air and natural materials. The boundaries between inside and outside are blurred.

- Room for Imagination: Users can interact and move walls around to make the house their own. The key green structure is presented as a blank canvas on which to build. Green fabrics from Knoll were used for the pillows and upholstery.

- Separation of Materials: When the house is mass-produced, the slotted construction allows easy assembly, disassembly, and shipping. All of the materials can be separated for recycling at the end of The Bamboo Loft's lifespan.

- Education of Users: A booklet of green materials used and where to find more information about these materials comes with the house.

bamboo
a renewable
resource

Fun Facts

There are many building products manufactured from recycled materials available on the market. Look for options that include recycled content tile, countertops, flooring, decking and wall panels. Alternative materials such as bamboo and cork are also becoming popular and have greatly reduced environmental impacts as compared to conventional flooring materials. Bamboo and cork are called rapidly renewable materials because they are so quick to grow.

Renewable Energy Award

The Patchwork Home – a Story
Anuradha Lingappa, Usha Lingappa, Krista Farey (San Francisco, CA)

One day when Grandma Josephine was young, she decided she needed a house for her family. Her husband, Grandpa Joe, wanted something unusual so they went down to Hobbiton but there were no houses for sale. "Fine," she said and she went to Napa and bought some land and decided to build her own house. The first thing that she noticed on her land was a river. She decided to not use the ordinary electric company's power. She made a water wheel. Then Grandma and Grandpa ran to SCRAP* to get some recycled building materials. They fit a lot of scraps together and built what they called their "Patchwork Home." They had two kids at the time. They were AnaSophia and Ellisa. Both girls were four years old. They needed more electricity, so they added a windmill on their land. They used straw bales because

AnaSophia had learned the word "green" and that gave Grandma Josephine an idea to make the house green. To get more electricity they put solar panels on the south roof and they did not pollute at all. They used the clothesline as a dryer and they hand washed everything. They made compost below the outhouse as garden fertilizer and grew their food around the house and on the living roof. When the girls grew up, Ellisa moved out and away and AnaSophia stayed with her parents and her husband and children. Everyone was happy – except their teenaged daughter who had laundry duty.

* Scroungers Center for Reusable Art Parts, San Francisco (SCRAP)
  is a store where you can buy used materials in California.

Fun Facts

Anuradha Lingappa, a sixth grader at Synergy School in San Francisco, was the youngest entrant in the competition! With the help of her sister and mother, she built the most colorful dollhouse we received and the only dollhouse that utilized three different types of renewable energy: wind, solar, and water. Can you find all three? This dollhouse, with its creative doll family that you will find while visiting Peter Whiteley's house later in the book, was part of Anuradha's Girl Scout Architecture and Environmental Design Badge.

Floor and Burners are pasta!

Shoebox Dollhouse

University of California Berkeley Extension class – Current Issues in Design, taught by Heather Ferguson. Students: Emily Geren, Mina Millet, Vantrung Nguyen, Kristen Nippa, Kathleen Roche Hubert, Renee Urbanowicz, Greg Walsh, Debbie Wong

Special thanks to the certified green builder who donated the superstructure for the shoebox dollhouse. It is made of scrap wood from the cabinet shop.

Concept Statement:

The dollhouse, each room made in a shoebox, brings us back to childhood when we would make theatres from the big boxes and reinvent new play things out of cast-away objects.

Shoeboxes, balsa wood, cardboard, glass, playing cards, and newspaper have been transformed into room materials.

This shoebox dollhouse was made with our hopes to raise awareness of recycled items and to encourage creativity.

The dollhouse exemplifies "green" sustainability through the materials that are actually used in the room as well as in the choice of material that they are intended to represent.

The balsa wood kitchen cabinets are stained with Ceylon tea, a natural product. The cabinet doors and drawers are intended to be made of walnut, a natural wood product.

A sample of a suede fabric, made from recycled plastics, is used to provide a soft, plush seat for the banquette in the dining room. The dining room table is made of recycled glass.

The bathroom floor is made of balsa wood. It represents bamboo – a rapidly reproducing wood product.

The rug on the 2nd floor bedroom/office is made of silk, a natural renewable resource.

Rooftop gardens should be more than just a beautiful retreat. The greening of rooftops can enhance air and climate quality and help combat "heat islands" - the altered micro-climates created by too few trees and greenery in dense urban spaces.

Perhaps in this day of toss-away plastic, our children and grandchildren can create a simpler creative playroom and enjoy the things that have been left behind.

Fun Facts

Since the 1950s, the size of the typical American home has grown dramatically, therefore increasing the amount of energy and resources used to provide us with shelter. One of the best ways to reduce environmental impact on new homes or remodels is to downsize. With good design, it is often possible to build a better home with less square footage and less cost than a conventional approach. We do not have to live in shoeboxes, but we certainly can do without giant homes!

Green Urban Award

The Skyscraper Dollhouse
Alfred Twu, University of Berkeley (Berkeley, CA)

Overview
With space running out in the Bay Area, it makes sense to build up rather than out. City living makes for less traffic and preserves open space.

Four floors each have a theme.

First Floor: the City
With a detailed façade, benches, and open walls, this building makes a welcoming addition to any doll city. There is a bus stop and train station all within a compact, space-saving footprint.

Second Floor: the Garden
Even in the most urban places, there is a place and a need for plants. Green roofs not only provide outdoor space, but also save energy.

Third Floor: the Home
Energy and resource conservation starts in the home. The dollhouse itself is made entirely from scrap wood.

Fourth Floor: the World
Caring for the world begins with knowing about the world and the way the natural environment works.

Fun Facts

The United States currently uses more energy for transportation than it does for buildings! This dollhouse won the Green Urban Award because it offers access to public transportation on its first floor. You can help reduce transportation energy use by taking the bus or train, riding a bike, carpooling, shopping close to home, and buying a car that gets good gas mileage.

Student Dollhouses

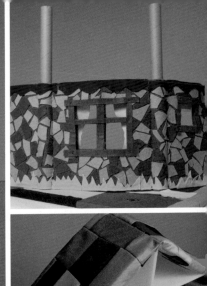

Build Your Own Green Dollhouse

Peter Whiteley's Dollhouse

By Peter Whiteley, Sunset Magazine

Let's face it. Children are tough on toys. Therefore, it was part of my design goals to build a dollhouse that was sturdy, attractive, and had rooms that could be easily reached. I also decided that the dollhouse had to use readily available materials and be designed so it could be built by a typical reader of the magazine for which I write–Sunset Magazine. This design decision meant only basic woodworking skills and common tools were needed.

Choice

I also wanted to leave the detailing of the little structure somewhat open ended so it would be easy to substitute different materials or finishes dependent upon what is locally available to the builder. I tried to use a wide variety of "green" products in the project so that children (and the parent builders) could discover the rich and wide range of materials that they could include in both a dollhouse or a full-sized home.

Some of the key products were:

Homosote paneling. I bought a 4- by 8-foot panel of 1/2-inch-thick Homosote at a local building supply store. This product, which is made with recycled paper, is used as the exterior walls and roof, and it plays the same role as SIPS (Structural Insulated Panels) does in a real house. This feature means no wood is used in most of the framing.

Natural Clay Plaster. In real life this integrally colored material from American Clay Products is used on interior walls. It is mixed with water and is applied in thin coats to walls to add rich color and texture. For the dollhouse, I used it on both exterior and interior wall surfaces.

Natural Clay Paint. A no-VOC paint made with clay also comes in a variety of earthy colors. This product is from Bio Shield. It has a chalky finish and can be used on accent walls, as I did in the dollhouse, or to paint an entire room.

Composite wood. These products are often made with recycled plastic and wood fiber. I cut a piece of Trex decking into 1/4-inch-thick slices to serve as the second floor deck.

Interior flooring and finishes. I used scrap pieces of bamboo flooring, left-over pieces of a handsome recycled panel called Kirei (made with twigs and branches of sorghum), Marmoleum, rubber floor tile, an FSC-certified hardwood (Ipe decking), and recycled-content rug. But I also had other choices: cork tile, Richlite (a paper-based surface), concrete tile, natural stone, recycled glass tile, cotton and wool fabrics, and organic wall paper as some other possibilities for the interior.

Other materials. Scrap pieces of plywood and straw board make the base, bottom floor frame and center wall. Sheet copper from a recycle yard is used for roofing. I found a sample of a wood-substitute floor product (Pergo) and synthetic slate as other exterior surfaces and, finally, I used sand mixed with wood glue as faux gravel in my landscape.

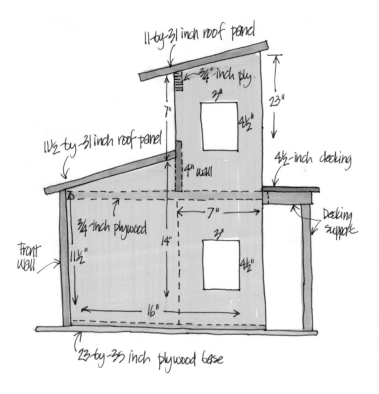

Roof panel labels (sketch):
- 11-by-31 inch roof panel
- 3/4-inch ply.
- 3"
- 4½"
- 23"
- 7"
- 11½-by-31 inch roof panel
- 4½-inch decking
- 4" wall
- 3/4 inch plywood
- 7"
- Decking support
- Front wall
- 11½"
- 14"
- 3"
- 4½"
- 16"
- 23-by-35 inch plywood base

Construction

The sketch to the left left shows the profile of the end and center walls of my dollhouse. The shape is totally arbitrary and can be changed to suit space and materials, but I did want to make a home that could integrate thoughtful solar design with deep overhanging roof lines that would be appropriate to this Western-style home.

Cut identical shapes from the Homosote for the two end walls, and one from the strawboard (or particle board) for the center wall. This center wall piece will rest on the plywood floor, so reduce its height by the thickness of the plywood. The center wall and the two flanking second-floor panels make a + shaped section that stiffens the whole house. (I made the floor pieces from Kirei, but any panel product or even recycled woods could be substituted). Cut shallow grooves in each side of the center wall so the floor panels can glue into them.

Cut openings for windows in the Homosote side walls, then glue and screw (or nail) the side pieces to the floor panel. Position center wall panel, check distance to side walls, and cut second floor panels to fit. Glue floor panels in shallow grooves, and attach with glue and screws running through side walls.

Measure and cut front wall section from Homosote. Cut window and door openings, then glue and nail or screw to front. Cut and add second-floor front wall sections. (I used shallow pieces of Kirei above window openings as symbolic glu-lam beams, pieces of plywood or Homosote could be used to do the same thing.)

Cut, glue, and attach the roof panels.

Ready to finish

After the glue has dried over night, you are ready to finish the house. Cut vertical pieces of flooring as the siding for the two-story section of the rear. Trace and cut openings for windows, score shallow saw-blade-wide grooves to make it look like vertical board-and-batten paneling, and glue in place.

Mix and add clay plaster to exterior and any interior walls you wish to finish with plaster. Paint remaining interior wall surfaces, then cut and add flooring pieces.

When surfaces are dried, lift and glue dollhouse to a piece of 23- by 35-inch plywood base. Cut and glue front and rear exterior patio surfaces. If a second-floor deck is wanted, add a ledger board across back of house and attach to floor panels. Build framing from scrap wood and attach composite-wood decking. Finish by mixing sand with wood glue, then apply to side "yard" with a wide putty blade.

Peter Whiteley's dollhouse decorated with furniture
and a dollhouse family from other dollhouses.

Make Your Own Re-Use Shoe Box Dollhouse

By Katrina Jones

Can't fit all of your new found-object furnishings in your old dollhouse? Maybe it is time to make a new one. With a bookshelf, some shoeboxes, and decorating materials, you can make your own dollhouse.

The House Structure

The great part about making your own dollhouse is that you can decide how many floors and rooms you want. Do you want four stories with one room on each floor or two stories with three rooms each? When you have decided how big you want your dollhouse to be, then you can go searching for the building structure – a bookshelf.

You may want to use a bookshelf that is lying around your house unused. Or, you can hunt for old bookshelves at garage sales and flea markets. Bookshelves with shelves that are at least twelve inches tall each work best with standard-size shoeboxes.

To make a room like the ones in the Shoebox House, all you need is:

MATERIALS:	TOOLS:
- a shoebox (lid and bottom)	- a glue gun (or duct tape)
- a piece of cardboard 12" by 12" (optional)	- scissors (optional)
- decorating materials	

The Rooms

Once you have your dollhouse structure, you need to make the individual rooms. Old shoeboxes are plentiful, and they make good-sized rooms. The dollhouse pictured above has six shoebox rooms.

Here are the steps you should follow:

1. Usually, the sides of a shoebox are glued together with little tabs. Gently pull the tabs to open one of the longer sides of the shoebox. Now you should have a shoebox with one of its longer sides open and the other one closed. The closed side is going to make the floor of the room; the open side is going to be part of the wall.

2. Set the box down so that the floor of the room is flat on your tabletop.

3. This step is optional. If you want, you can use the 12" by 12" piece of cardboard to stabilize the wall side of the shoe-

box. To do this, you should cut the cardboard to the size of wall side that is made of what was the bottom of the box plus the side of the box that you opened. Then glue or tape the cardboard piece to the wall side of the room.

4. Now, you should set the shoebox lid down in front of the closed or floor side of the shoebox room. Set the lid down so that the inside of the lid is facing up and one long side of the lid is beside the long floor side of the room.

5. Gently pull open the tabs on the long side of the lid that is lined up with the floor side of the room.

6. Glue or tape the open side of the lid to the floor side of the room. The lid is now the other half of the floor.

7. Finally, you can paint your room or glue in "wallpaper" and add some of the found-object furnishings you made.

Found-Object Furnishings

By Katrina Jones

Need a new look for that dollhouse dining room? Have a bunch of old film canisters that you do not know how to use? Not sure what to do with that one slipper left from the pair grandma gave you? Feel like there has to be some useful purpose for your sister's matchbox collection? Maybe it is time for you to think about found-object furnishings.

You may be wondering, "What is a found-object?" Good question. A found-object is something lying around your house, yard, or street that you could use in a new way.

For example:
- Checkers from a game board can double as dinner plates for your dolls.
- A cancelled stamp on a letter from your aunt could be re-used as a picture on the wall of your dollhouse.
- You could use an old brass knob from a dresser drawer as a fake lamp in your doll's living room.

Why should we use found-objects in dollhouses?

1. Well, it's fun. Re-using old stuff this way adds a personal touch (and sometimes a bit of humor) to your dollhouse. For example, re-using an empty container that held bathtub cleaner to make a bathtub.

2. Using found-objects encourages creativity and ingenuity. You use creative thinking skills to help you decide what objects you could use to make a dining room table or to think of all the different ways you could use empty film canisters to make additions to your dollhouse.

3. Re-using objects keeps them from being thrown away and ending up in landfills.

4. It saves money. By re-using objects you already have, or can find easily, you can fill a whole dollhouse with furniture for free.

Some of the people who made the dollhouses in this book used old found-objects to create new, cheap, fun furniture. Let's take a look at these creative inventions!

For the Dining Room and Living Room

Helpful Tip
The following project is most easily done with at least two people. One should preferably be an adult or an older child who can safely handle a glue gun or box cutters.

Tables

The CD Table pictured here is from the Mobile Living dollhouse (see pages 36-37). Some artists have used junk-mail compact discs in their artwork because the CDs have a nice shine and they are a plentiful, man-made resource. Unfortunately, since they are so plentiful, they are rapidly piling up in landfills. Re-using these CDs for art projects helps cut down the number of them that are thrown into the trash.

After you gather your materials, here are the steps you should follow:

1. First, plug in the glue gun so it has time to heat up. Be careful not to burn yourself when you are holding the glue gun.

2. While the glue gun is heating, you can make the table's legs. Along one four-inch side of one piece of wood, measure two inches in and make a mark with your pencil. From this mark, draw a line that extends one and one half inches into the center of the piece of wood. Try to make this line perpendicular to the top edge. Use the box cutter to cut along the line you have made. Cut away a little of the wood on each side of the line, so that you will

To make a table like this one, all you need is:

MATERIALS:	TOOLS:
- 2 CDs (for the tabletop)	- a glue gun
- 2 pieces of balsa wood (for legs) (Dimensions: 4 inches long x 3 inches tall x ½ inch thick)	- a ruler
	- 3 clothespins
	- a pencil
	- a box cutter with a safety blade
	- an adult (to help)

have a slit in the wood that is approximately 1½ inches down into the wood and ½ an inch across. Measure and cut the other piece of wood this same way. Interlock the two pieces of wood at the slits. By now, the glue gun should be ready.

3. To make the tabletop, lay one CD on a table with its shiny side facing down. Place a few drops of glue around the top of the CD. Lay the second CD on top of the first one with its shiny side facing up. It is like making a CD and glue sandwich. Line up the two CDs the way you would line up two pieces of sandwich bread. Watch out for glue squeezing out the sides like extra mustard! The glue will be really hot, and it could burn you if you touch it.

4. Use the clothespins to hold the two CDs together until the glue dries.

5. Once the CD-glue sandwich dries, you are ready to attach the legs. Lay the tabletop you have made down and set the interlocked legs on top of it. Hold the legs and tabletop still while a second individual carefully spreads glue along the edges where the tabletop meets the wood. Hold the legs in place for a minute or two.

6. After fifteen to twenty minutes, everything should be dry and you can flip the table over onto its legs. Decorate the top with permanent markers, or set the table for dinner and call your dolls to come eat!

This CD-table used balsa wood for legs, but you could use any type of scrap wood. Or, you could use something completely different. The CD-table in the Rosaceae Sustainus dollhouse used metal nuts and bolts to make a table leg. Spools of thread, thumbtacks, golf tees, or pen caps can be used to make legs for tables or chairs. Can you think of any other found-objects from your house that you could use

to make table legs? What about tabletops? Besides CDs, you could use a jar lid, a stationary box, or a case for an audiocassette. What else?

Chairs

Now that your dolls have a table on which to place their dinner, they need some chairs to sit on at their table. The creator of the Patchwork Home came up with a simple answer to this problem. Film canisters make quick, easy dining room stools. You can decorate the outside with glitter or stickers and you can even put things inside them.

Zebra-print fabric, cotton stuffing, and plastic tops from spray cans were used to make unique chairs for a low table in Mobile Living. In the Shoebox Dollhouse, champagne corks have been covered with fake leather fabric and wire to make the chairs by the kitchen counter.

To make a bathtub like the one in the Monopoly House, all you need is:

MATERIALS:	TOOLS:
- a spray bottle	- a glue gun
- 4 plastic bottle caps (for legs)	- scissors
- a wooden skewer or dowel	- a hole-punch
- a piece of plastic or fabric	- a box cutter with a safety blade
- duct tape	- a marker

For the Kitchen and Bathroom

Kitchen Appliances

Save the foil that your lunch was wrapped in, wash it, and re-use it! In the kitchen of the Shoebox Dollhouse, aluminum foil was used to give kitchen appliances a metallic look. The stovetop, sink basin, and refrigerator have been covered with scraps of aluminum foil. The ventilation system is a toilet paper roll covered with aluminum foil.

Sinks

Can you tell what the faucet for the sink in the Shoebox Dollhouse is made from? It's a paper clip! Can you think of any other things you could use to make a faucet?

That sink basin was made from aluminum foil, but many other things could work too. Do you have any shells from visiting the beach? The Patchwork Home has a bathroom sink made from a shell and some clay.

Bathtubs and Showers

The creators of the Monopoly House made a bathtub from part of a spray bottle. Many of the spray bottles that contain household cleaners are made of plastic that can be recycled. Sometimes these bottles are still made with types of plastic that cannot be recycled. These bottles cannot be re-used to hold other types of liquid because of the chemicals they contained. However, if the bottles are washed out thoroughly then they may be able to be used for art projects. Make sure it is okay for you to use a specific bottle.

Here are the steps you should follow:

1. Have an appropriate person plug in the glue gun, and remember not to touch either the hot end of the glue gun or the glue.

2. While the glue gun is heating, you can work on the shower curtain. Use the scissors to cut the fabric or plastic into a rectangle that looks like the right size for the bathtub you

are going to make. Along one of the longer sides of the rectangle, put five or six holes in a row for the "curtain rod" (the wooden skewer). Slide the curtain rod through the holes and attach it to the walls of your dollhouse's bathroom with some hot glue.

3. Decide what size and shape you want your bathtub to be. Use a permanent marker to draw a line around the spray bottle to show which part will become the bathtub. Use the box cutter to cut along the line you have made.

4. After the bottle is cut, it may have sharp edges. Please be careful. Place some duct tape along the cut edge of the bathtub to make sure it will not cut you while you are playing. In the Monopoly House, the plastic coating from a computer cord was used to safeguard the ragged edge. However, there are some computer parts that should not be handled without proper equipment, and duct tape is widely available to use as a protective covering.

5. For the legs of your bathtub, you could use small pieces of plastic like the ones in the picture or a variety of other objects. Can you think of some other possibilities? What about plastic bottle caps? Whatever you use, simply glue them to the bottom of the bathtub and then glue them to the floor of your dollhouse. Or, you can glue the bathtub in without using any legs.

The Animal House used a small baking tin to make a bathtub instead of using a spray bottle. Can you think of any other things in your house that you could use to make a bathtub?

To make a dresser like the one here, all you need is:

MATERIALS:	TOOLS:
7 matchboxes	regular glue
7 small beads	
4 push pins	

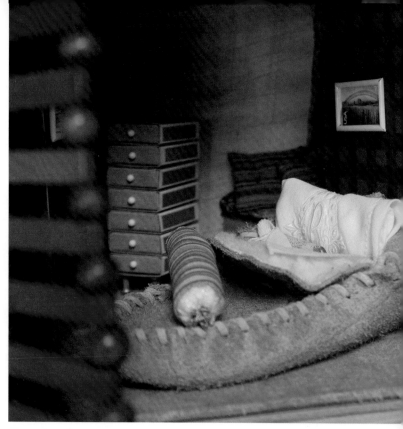

For the Bedroom

Beds

After she eats dinner at the CD-table and brushes her teeth in the shell sink, your doll will need a place to snuggle down to sleep. What can you use to make a bed for her? Maybe a stationary box, a plastic tray from a box of cookies, or something else. The Animal House has a bed made from an old slipper. Maybe someone lost the other one.

Nightstands

Besides the bed, bedrooms often have nightstands with lamps. With a lamp your doll can read a bedtime story before she goes to sleep. In the Animal House, a three-legged plastic support from a pizza box functions as a nightstand. A knob from a drawer acts as a lamp.

Dresser Drawers

Empty matchboxes make great drawers. You can glue several of them together in rows and columns to make a large dresser, or you can glue them one on top of another in a single row like the one in the Animal House.

Here are the steps you should follow:

1. Glue one small bead to the front of each matchbox. These beads will act as drawer knobs. Make sure you put them on a side that pulls out of the box easily.

2. Now glue the matchboxes to each other stacking each one on top of the other.

3. After the glue between the boxes has dried, push the four push pins into the bottom matchbox.

4. Decorate your dresser and put your doll's clothes or toys inside it.

Project Credits

Original Project Team

Once the idea was hatched, this is the team that made sure it got off the ground!

- o Jill Boone, County of San Mateo RecycleWorks
- o Ruth Peterson, Sustainable San Mateo County
- o Jennifer Roberts, author of *Good Green Homes*
- o Peter Whiteley, Senior Writer for Sunset Magazine
- o Lisa Boquieren, San Francisco Design Center
- o Pat Koblenz, Coyote Point Museum
- o Ellen Newman, Public Relations
- o Eric Rohlfing, Topos Architects

Early Helpful Friends

Once we got going, these friends donated valuable services.

- o Stephie Tucker, website design and maintenance, iKorb Inc.
- o Madeleine Corson, logo and early design, Madeleine Corson Design
- o Bill Smith, e-list service, Savicom
- o Got.net, web hosting
- o Gina Blus, project management
- o Judy Williams, administrative services, Sustainable San Mateo County
- o Beals Martin, Inc., free warehouse space
- o Eric Corey Freed, publicity and networking, Organic Architect
- o Miriam Reiter, Malia Langworthy, and Tracie Bills, for helping out whenever they were needed, RecycleWorks
- o The Menlo Park Firemen who rescued Jill at the warehouse one night when the roll-up door would not close – and the San Mateo County Public Works team who repaired the door the next day.
- o Our friends next door who wish to remain anonymous but who opened our warehouse for the delivery services and allowed us to use their bathroom on the days we were working at the warehouse all day!

Book and Exhibition Team

This group made the book, the museum exhibit and related events happen!

- o Emily Hagopian, photographer, Essential Images
- o Katrina Jones, curator and exhibit designer
- o Jason F. McLennan, Ecotone Publishing
- o Stuart Butler, construction
- o Shellie's Miniature Mania for loaning us dolls and props for the dollhouse photography, including one lawyer that sells for $400 and can be seen waiting for a bus in the Skyscraper Dollhouse photos.
- o Carl Oosterman and Michelle Martin, Coyote Point Museum
- o Pam Brown, Lillian Clark, Ann Edminster, Francie Allen, events
- o Susan Hemmenway, Graphic Lab, graphic design
- o Erin Gehle, Book Design

Competition Friends

This group made the competition and jury event successful.

- o Eric Rohlfing, jury event coordinator
- o Laura Ingall, Tracie Bills, Cristie Boone and Curtis Boone who helped unpack the dollhouses and move them around.
- o Pro Line Painters for painting the wall in the warehouse a sky blue – to enhance the background for the jury event.
- o AIA, San Francisco and San Mateo County Chapters; USGBC, Northern California Chapter; and Architects/Designers/ Planners for Social Responsibility for helping to announce the competition.
- o Kim Lessard, California College of the Arts, publicity for writing a press release to announce the 11 winning dollhouses.
- o County of San Mateo for loaning us tables, lights, etc.

Jurors

- o David Arkin, Arkin Tilt Architects and his daughter, Ellie Arkin
- o Sharon Refvem, board member with the U.S. Green Building Council Northern California Chapter and architect with Hawley Peterson & Snyder with her son, Tom Kaheli
- o Shellie Kazan, dollhouse expert and owner of Shellie's Miniature Mania in San Carlos with a young dollhouse collector, Katie Rupert
- o Abigail Peterson of Sunset Magazine with young friend, Jeanette Chow
- o Martina Scanlan of Interiors and Sources with daughter, Kellen Scanlan
- o Jennifer Roberts, author of Good Green Homes with young friend, Chiara Tice
- o Topher Delaney, environmental artist and builder with Stephanie Hildago.

Friendly Businesses and Sponsors

Without financial assistance and in-kind donations, this project would not have happened. Special thanks to all of the following businesses for their support:

- o County of San Mateo RecycleWorks
- o Sustainable San Mateo County
- o San Francisco Department of the Environment
- o Alameda County Waste Management Authority
- o Hayward Lumber
- o Eco Design Resources
- o BFI / Allied Waste Industries
- o Norcal Waste Systems of San Mateo County
- o Whole House Building Supply
- o South Bayside Waste Management Authority
- o Janet Lowrey Smith

And with deep appreciation to this group of green architectural and professional firms for their support of our project, their energy and volunteer time, and their continuing determination to educate as well as design outstanding green buildings.

o 450 Architects

o Anderson Brule Architects

Project Credits continued:

o Andrea Traber Architecture + Sustainability

o Goody Clancy

o Group 4 Architects

o Hermannsson Architects

o HOK

o Laura Schwartz & Associates

o Murdock Young Architects

o Sou-ou Planning Consultants Inc.

o Stahnke Kitagawa Architects

o Tony Garza Architect

o URS Corporation

o WGS

Media Partners

o Sunset Magazine

o Interiors & Sources

o Ecotone Publishing

Willimena the Watchdog Saves the Earth by Brenna Smith and Kiyomi Troemner that was submitted with the Monopoly Manor Dollhouse.

About Ecotone Publishing
The Green Building Publisher

Ecotone is an independent publishing company whose mission is to educate and provide examples of restorative design to people in the building industry. In nature, an ecotone is a biologically rich transition zone between two or more dissimilar ecosystems. For architecture, it is about understanding the richness of the boundaries between the habitats of people and the environment. Ecotone – exploring the relationship between the built and natural environments.

For more information on Ecotone or to purchase other books please visit our website at:
www.ecotonedesign.com

or contact us at:
Ecotone LLC
P.O. Box 7147
Kansas City, Missouri
64113-0147

e-mail: info@ecotonedesign.com